Pebble®
Plus
Bilingüe/
Bilingual

Máquinas maravillosas/Mighty Machines

Bombarderos/Bombers

por/by Jennifer Reed

Traducción/Translation: Dr. Martín Luis Guzmán Ferrer

Editor Consultor/Consulting Editor: Dra. Gail Saunders-Smith

Consultor/Consultant: Raymond L. Puffer, PhD
U.S. Air Force Historian
Edwards Air Force Base, California

Capstone
press®

Mankato, Minnesota

Pebble Plus is published by Capstone Press,
151 Good Counsel Drive, P.O. Box 669, Mankato, Minnesota 56002.
www.capstonepress.com

1 2 3 4 5 6 13 12 11 10 09 08

Library of Congress Cataloging-in-Publication Data
Reed, Jennifer, 1967–
    [Bombers. Spanish & English]
    Bombarderos = Bombers / por/by Jennifer Reed.
    p. cm. — (Máquinas maravillosas) (Mighty machines)
    Pebble Plus bilingüe/bilingual.
    Includes index.
    Text in Spanish and in English.
    ISBN-13: 978-1-4296-2376-6 (hardcover)
    ISBN-10: 1-4296-2376-4 (hardcover)
    1. Bombers — Juvenile literature. I. Title. II. Title: Bombers.
UG1242.B6R4418 2008
623.74'63 — dc22
    2008001253

Summary: Brief text and photographs describe bombers, their parts, and what they do — in both English
    and Spanish.

Editorial Credits
Mari Schuh and Erika L. Shores, editors; Katy Kudela, bilingual editor; Eida del Risco, Spanish copy editor;
    Patrick D. Dentinger, book designer; Jo Miller, photo researcher

Photo Credits
DVIC/MSGT Paul J. Harrington, 4–5; TSGT Richard Freeland, 1, 19
George Hall/Check Six, 8–9
Photo by Ted Carlson/Fotodynamics, cover, 6–7, 10–11, 15, 16–17
U.S. Air Force, 13; Master Sgt. Lance Cheung, 20–21

Note to Parents and Teachers

The Máquinas maravillosas/Mighty Machines set supports national social studies standards related to science, technology, and society. This book describes and illustrates bombers in both English and Spanish. The images support early readers in understanding the text. The repetition of words and phrases helps early readers learn new words. This book also introduces early readers to subject-specific vocabulary words, which are defined in the Glossary section. Early readers may need assistance to read some words and to use the Table of Contents, Glossary, Internet Sites, and Index sections of the book.

Table of Contents

Tabla de contenidos

What Are Bombers?

Bombers are big airplanes.
They drop bombs on targets
during battles.

¿Qué son los bombarderos?

Los bombarderos son unos
aviones grandes. En las batallas
tiran bombas sobre los blancos.

4

Some bombers fly high
in the sky. They are
hard for enemies to see.

Algunos bombarderos vuelan
muy alto en el cielo. Es difícil
que los enemigos puedan verlos.

Parts of Bombers

Bombers have fast engines.

Engines push bombers

through the air.

Las partes de
los bombarderos

Los bombarderos tienen

unos motores muy rápidos.

Los motores impulsan a

los bombarderos por el aire.

Bombers have computers.
The crew uses computers
to find targets.

Los bombarderos tienen
computadoras. La tripulación
usa las computadoras para
encontrar los blancos.

11

The bomb bay holds bombs.

The bay doors open and

bombs drop to the ground.

La bahía de bombas contiene

las bombas. Las puertas

de la bahía se abren y

las bombas caen a la tierra.

bomb bay/
bahía de bombas

Bomber Crews

Pilots fly bombers.

A pilot and copilot

sit in the cockpit.

Las tripulaciones de los bombarderos

Los pilotos pilotan

los bombarderos.

El piloto y el copiloto

están en la cabina.

Crew members have
different jobs on bombers.
The navigator tells
the pilot where to fly.

Los miembros de la tripulación
tienen diferentes trabajos en
los bombarderos. El navegador
le dice al piloto por dónde
debe volar.

Another crew member
makes sure bombs
hit their targets.

Otro miembro de
la tripulación hace
que las bombas den
en los blancos.

Mighty Machines

Bombers protect the country during battles. Bombers are mighty machines.

Máquinas maravillosas

Los bombarderos protegen a un país en las batallas. Los bombarderos son máquinas maravillosas.

Glossary

battle — a fight between two groups

bomb — an object that blows up when it hits a target

cockpit — the space at the front of an airplane where pilots control the airplane

copilot — a person who helps the pilot fly an airplane

crew— a team of people who work together

navigator — a person who tells the pilot where to fly

pilot — a person who flies an airplane

target — something that is aimed at or shot at

Glosario

la batalla — lucha entre dos bandos

el blanco — objeto al que se le apunta o dispara

la bomba — objeto que estalla cuando pega en el blanco

la cabina — espacio en el frente del avión desde donde los pilotos controlan el avión

el copiloto — persona que ayuda al piloto a pilotar el avión

el navegador — persona que le dice al piloto por dónde volar

el piloto — persona que maneja o pilota un avión

la tripulación — grupo de personas que trabaja en equipo

Internet Sites

FactHound offers a safe, fun way to find Internet sites related to this book. All of the sites on FactHound have been researched by our staff.

Here's how:

1. Visit *www.facthound.com*

2. Choose your grade level.

3. Type in this book ID **1429623764** for age-appropriate sites. You may also browse subjects by clicking on letters, or by clicking on pictures and words.

4. Click on the **Fetch It** button.

FactHound will fetch the best sites for you!

Index

Sitios de Internet

FactHound te brinda una manera divertida y segura de encontrar sitios de Internet relacionados con este libro. Hemos investigado todos los sitios de FactHound. Es posible que algunos sitios no estén en español.

Se hace así:

1. Visita *www.facthound.com*

2. Elige tu grado escolar.

3. Introduce este código especial **1429623764** para ver sitios apropiados a tu edad, o usa una palabra relacionada con este libro para hacer una búsqueda general.

4. Haz un clic en el botón **Fetch It**.

¡FactHound buscará los mejores sitios para ti!

Índice